Knowing
& Growing

Knowing & Growing

A Lent
course to
lengthen
our lives

DAVID ADAM

kevin
mayhew

First published in 2003 by

KEVIN MAYHEW LTD
Buxhall, Stowmarket, Suffolk, IP14 3BW
E-mail: info@kevinmayhewltd.com

KINGSGATE PUBLISHING INC
1000 Pannell Street, Suite G, Columbia, MO 65201
E-mail: sales@kingsgatepublishing.com

9 8 7 6 5 4 3 2 1 ט

ISBN 1 84417 177 9
Catalogue No. 1500666

Cover design by Angela Selfe
Edited by Marian Reid
Typesetting by Fiona Connell-Finch
Printed and bound in Great Britain

Contents

DAVID ADAM was the Vicar of Lindisfarne, off the Northumbrian coast, for thirteen years until he retired in March 2003. His work involved ministering to thousands of pilgrims and other visitors. He is the author of many inspiring books on spirituality and prayer, and his Celtic writings have rekindled a keen interest in our Christian heritage.

Introduction

Early spring is always an exciting time: suddenly winter is past; the days lengthen, the sun strengthens, the birds sing and begin their nest-making. The garden comes alive again. The aconites and snowdrops are the heralds of spring. It is the time for pruning. Many plants are improved by being cut back, and careful pruning produces healthier and better plants. If left to themselves, they can become gnarled and twisted and don't produce the fruit or flower they are capable of producing. Other plants need to be split, divided up and replanted, and some of these can be given away. Plants, like people, thrive if they are not fighting for the same space, or if they are not in a space that has been used over and over: spring is also a time to add some nourishment to the land.

I tell you this, for I see Lent as a time of lengthening and letting the Son's power strengthen in our lives. If it is a time for cutting back, it is so that we can live fuller and more abundant lives, or so that we can have more to give away. I worry about the people who give up something for no purpose other than the fact that it is a Lenten tradition to do so. I once lived with a community who did not eat meat on Wednesdays or Fridays in Lent but instead ate salmon and cod, which were much more expensive. Just like a young niece of mine, who gave up sweets and moved on to chocolate. I do not see Lent as a time of misery or pointless renunciation, but as a time of growth and hope. I do not ask people, 'What are you giving up for Lent?', I ask them, 'What are you doing for Lent?' I worry in the same way about people who boast, 'I do not smoke, I do not drink, I do not swear', and add a whole list of self-righteous 'I do not's. I always want to ask them, 'What do you do? How do you live life to the full? How do you achieve the glory you were created for?' All that pruning is only truly productive if it leads to growth and to fullness of life.

This book is for those who want to explore the way to abundant life, for all those who seek to know Christ and the power of his resurrection (Philippians 3:10-11). The eight weeks of study are aimed at bringing us before the great mysteries of God as revealed in Christ Jesus. Therefore we are not so much required to talk about God as to bow before Him and to talk to Him. It is a book for all of us who are finding life hard, who are discovering that we are not where we want to be, or are not as perceptive as we thought we were. It is meant to be an 'extension course', not merely to extend our knowledge, though we shall do this, but rather to extend ourselves and our way of living and worshipping.

When my Uncle Bob returned from World War Two, he gave me a khaki-covered New Testament. Inside the front cover was the text from John 3:16: 'God so loved . . . that he gave his only begotten Son, to the end that all who believe in him should not perish, but have everlasting life.' The gap in the text was for you to write your name in. My uncle had never dared, but I did! This was a simple beginning for me, the start of discovering that God seeks a personal relationship with me. God cares for each of us as individuals – not because we deserve it, but out of his grace and love. So often in this world we are 'perishers', with bits being knocked off us, and often we feel fragile. God does not want this, he wants us to have life and life eternal. You might like to write out the text from John 3:16 and to insert your own name into it. Then take a little time to let the truth of this wonderful fact enter your heart and mind. We need to discover the fullness of life and life eternal that God offers us.

I used to visit my wife Denise when she was doing her teacher training at Alnwick Castle. At that time, it was a teacher training college, whereas now it is the setting for the Harry Potter films. I would see the shield and motto for the college – the words were from John 10:10: '*Ut vitam habeant et abundantius*' ('That they may have life, and have it abundantly'). What more could you desire for your students? Obviously this would only happen through Jesus Christ. The Christian God is not a God of restrictions but of fulfilment. Becoming a Christian is not about accepting a book of rules that will diminish you but about having a personal relationship with the living God who gives you life in all its fullness.

This is not to invest in historic research of the past, nor to project all our hopes and fears into the future. It is to live with an ever-present, loving God. This awareness will enrich our understanding of the past and our hope for the future; it will encourage us to explore both with greater hope and understanding.

With these thoughts in mind, I see Lent as time for change, a change of direction, which is best described as a 'repentance' or a 'turning around'. What we need is a change of attitude – a move from a historic understanding of God to a personal relationship, usually referred to as 'faith', and a change of heart which is an embracing of a newness of life, becoming a 'new creation'. So you will be faced with life-changing and life-challenging events. You should only venture further if you desire this and are willing to be changed.

Very little changes without planning and effort. I heard of a local minister who was asked by a lazy farmer to pray for his crops. The minister said, 'They need manure before I pray for them!' God in his grace gives to us abundantly, but he will not supply us with the things we should be doing ourselves. If we want a nice garden, we have to work at it. Similarly, if we want a better and more fruitful life, we have to work at it. A garden left on its own will go to ruin, it may take years, but its beauty and goodness will gradually be lost. A lot of people say they do what comes naturally when it comes to their daily living, but doing what comes naturally produces weeds and briars. If we want to have a full and productive life we have to put some planning and effort into it. A wise old man once said to me, 'Plan your work and work your plan.' At the time, he was talking about a garden, but I knew he meant me to relate it to the whole of my life. This Lent I intend to share with you a little of my planning and working, an approach to the Scriptures which has been tried and tested and which has brought results.

LECTIO DIVINA

When I was at college, I learned a way of reading Scripture which has stood me in good stead for the whole of my life since – though I do vary it a lot. This is called the 'Lectio Divina' or, more simply,

'Holy Reading' or 'Divine Reading'. This reading is divided into parts, which you are meant to follow, though there is always the freedom to stay with one part or to go backwards and forwards as you so desire. We had a regular time and place each day for Holy Reading, and we committed ourselves to it. This wasn't so much study as prayer, but it enriched our studies and, in turn, our studies often enriched it. I would like to offer you this pattern for Lent and beyond, preferably prayed in a group. I cannot emphasise enough the need for a regular, fixed time and place for prayer and meditation. I believe we all need a special holy place, for only then do all places become holy. The pattern for Holy Reading is as follows:

REALISE that you are in the presence of God. Be 'still and know'. Call upon him. Sit quietly in his presence. Ask for his guidance. I will suggest hymns and prayers for the start of each session. A time of silence is also of great importance. We need time to come before our God who is ever with us. Awareness of this reality is of the utmost importance. Use this period to relax. Make sure you are sitting comfortably. Let go of all tension in your body and mind. Breath gently and deeply. Let go and let God.

READ the passage chosen for the day. This need not be a long passage. Sometimes a verse will do. If you are alone it is better to read it out loud. Repeat important words and ideas and let them reverberate. Concentrate on the words and let them sink deep into your consciousness, do not let other thoughts or distractions crowd them out. To make it easier for you, the passage of Scripture for each week has been printed in full. But it is good to use a Bible and to become familiar with where the various books in it are in relationship to each other, so bring one with you and find the reading in it. It is good for someone other than the leader of the group to read the passage, as the more that can be shared around the better.

RUMINATE. Many of the early saints suggested we chew over the words. The Venerable Bede suggested we ruminate when dealing with the Scriptures. Too often, things are rushed in order to get on with what's next. Chew over the words, extract their goodness and 'digest' them. Before you begin this you may like to pray the ancient prayer:

> Blessed Lord, who has caused all Holy Scriptures to be written for our learning: grant that we may in such wise hear them, read, mark, learn, and inwardly digest them, that by patience and comfort of thy holy Word, we may embrace and ever hold fast the blessed hope of everlasting life, which thou hast given us in our Saviour Jesus Christ.

As you chew over the story or words, where do you see yourself in this situation? Use all your senses. Visualise what you have read. What images does it create? Bring each of your senses into play. Are there things you can see, touch, hear and smell? Can you see yourself in what has been read? If not, why not? Remember you are ruminating: take your time. This part of the Divine Reading is called meditation. The Hebrew word for meditate is 'hagah', and it means to whisper softly or to recite. If your mind wants to wander, pick out key words and recite them. Heed the guidance of St Paul in Philippians 4:4, 8. 'Rejoice in the Lord always; again I will say, Rejoice . . . whatever is true, whatever is honourable, whatever is just, whatever is pure, whatever is pleasing, whatever is commendable, if there is any excellence and if there is anything worthy of praise, think about these things.'

RESPOND to what you have just experienced. Respond towards God in prayer and thanksgiving. Respond towards your neighbour, the world, yourself. What is called for out of what you have received? What fruits of action does it demand? Jesus spoke in parables, not for us to study them, but so that we could respond to them. This part of the Holy Reading is called 'Oratio'. I used to confuse this with Oratorio, and it is not all that wrong. Let the music of the words resound in your inner being until they move you. As a more exact title of this section might be 'Prayer', it is important that you keep in communication with your God. I think of the words 'to work is to pray and to pray is to work'. Prayer is to be seen in action. Not only do we say, 'Your will be done', but we also have to seek to do God's will. When we are in groups, this section has two parts: a silent part, where we speak and listen to God, and then a part where we communicate with each other. Both these sections demand undivided attention. Group work is of great importance. Those who do not really listen carefully to others are unlikely to give God their undivided attention.

REST AND REJOICE. After the hard work and concentration of each session, make sure you have some time to enjoy what you have experienced and to enjoy the presence of each other. Be aware of where you are and whom you are with. Appreciate your surroundings and the generosity of your host. You should make sure you know all the members of your group. It is good to be able to thank people for their insight and sharing. We ought to be able to show we are genuinely interested in the people we are with.

This, like the last section, has two parts: after communicating with each other, turn to the ever-present God and rejoice in him. Just as with lovers, there is no need for words. Rest in his power, his peace and his love. This can be compared to sunbathing – lie back in the presence and just enjoy being there. Wallow in the reality that you are in the heart of God and that God is in your heart. I like the words of Albert Einstein: 'The most beautiful experience we can have is the mysterious.' Quietly rejoice in the fact that we dwell in him and he in us.

It is good to end this session with music and prayer. For this reason I have suggested hymns and prayers to end with, and I have purposely ended each session with a blessing. Blessings express the reality of the love of God towards us. They are not so much requests for a blessing as an acknowledgement that God does bless us.

So ends the session. But it is good to come away gently.

RECOLLECT. Bring together what has been done: seek to reap the harvest and to be fed by the Word of God. Take away with you a thought, a text or a resolution to use during the week. If you can have a short prayer or a sentence you are able to use during the days ahead, it could help to let your new awareness sink home. Recollect once or twice each day the presence of God and his love towards you. There is a lovely story from *Hebridean Altars* of a princess of the Isles. She had given food and shelter to one of the wandering saints. As he left he asked her, 'Tell me the secret of your exceeding gentleness.' At this, the lady mused for a long time, her eyes downcast; then she answered softly, as one waking from a lovely dream, 'There is no secret – only that I am always at his feet, and he is always in my heart.'

I have suggested short prayers and texts which might be of help, but it is important to have your own. You might like to bring a prayer to each session to pray quietly or to offer to the group.

It is useful for the leader to have a rough idea of how long each section should be. It is of the utmost importance that we are good timekeepers. Although some in the group may have all the time in the world, others will feel pressurised if the session goes on too long. The leader needs to be a good timekeeper, but should also have the ability to decide if a session needs shortening or lengthening. An approximate idea of timing follows, with the whole session lasting about an hour:

REALISE	10 minutes
READ	5-10 minutes
RUMINATE	in silence 10-15 minutes
RESPOND	in two sections: 20 minutes group session, then 2 minutes silence, leading into the next section
REST AND REJOICE	continue the silence for another 3-5 minutes; final prayers, music and blessing 5-10 minutes

If anyone does not have a copy of this book, it is good to let them know the readings for the session in advance and also any resources or illustrations they should try and bring with them.

Each week of Lent, we will look at one of the parables of Jesus. Ash Wednesday and Easter Day have extra readings relevant to the day. On Ash Wednesday, we will look at our approach to the whole of Lent. On Easter Day, we will rejoice in the mystery of the resurrection. The whole of the approach to Lent can be summarised in the words of Gerard Manley Hopkins in his poem *The Wreck of the Deutschland*: 'Let him easter in us, be a dayspring to the dimness of us', or in the words of St Paul: 'I want to know Christ and the power of his resurrection' (Philippians 3:10).

I have chosen the parables because of the simple pictures they create while also exposing us to deep mysteries and challenges. We can just look at the picture on the surface or focus in a new way and look more deeply. Some of the 'Magic Eye' books and paintings show us we can focus in more ways than one on a subject, so seeing deeper and further. Every time we extend ourselves to reach beyond the obvious and the immediate, we are reaching towards a higher awareness and potential. Above all, the parables call for immediate responses more than for analysis or comment. The parables want you to do something. They call for a change.

I have assumed that each member of the group will have a copy of this book. It is better to have worked through a session at least once before coming together, as the leader will probably have worked through the session at least once. At the beginning of each session, I have suggested something you could bring with you to illustrate what the session is about. These illustrations could be used during the discussion time or as a preparation for the opening of the meeting, thus providing a good warm-up and lead-in to the time of realisation and prayer. In the same way, the group might like to suggest music or prayers for the opening session to the leader, though preferably before the meeting. It will be necessary to have a CD or tape player for each session. A keyboard could prove useful as well. If there is no way to play music, you can either read out the hymns, or sing them unaccompanied.

I want to emphasise that this is the life that God has given us. This is the life he wants us to live. We should not leave for another world what God wants us to do in this one. If you believe in eternal life, as I do, you must realise that you are already in it now. It is you, and what you have made of yourself, who rises beyond death, not another person. Take to heart the words of Boris Pasternak in his novel *Doctor Zhivago*: 'Man is born to live, not to prepare for life.'

DAVID ADAM

WEEK 1: ASH WEDNESDAY
Don't Give Up!

Resources

Bring cuttings from newspapers of stories of people whose lives appear to be empty and vacuous. Bring a positive Lent rule, or resolution, which you will try and keep. Do not make the resolution too hard, but at the same time it ought to stretch you in some way.

REALISE

(10 minutes)

Hymn

I, the Lord of sea and sky
Or: Change my heart, Lord
Or: Fill thou my life, O Lord my God
Or: Forty days and forty nights

After the music, keep a short time of silence and, within it, affirm that you are in the presence of God. Know that he loves you and gives you himself. Seek to be aware of the reality of God in your life. To live without regard to him is to live a lie.

> O Gracious and Holy Father, give us
> wisdom to perceive you,
> diligence to seek you,
> patience to wait for you,
> eyes to behold you,
> a heart to meditate upon you,
> a life to proclaim you:
> through the power of the Spirit
> of Jesus Christ our Lord. Amen.
>
> *(St Benedict)*

Lord, lead us today
to a greater awareness,
to a firmer grasp of reality,
to a wider vision,
to a deeper sensitivity
to a response to wonder
and to a constant love for you.

READ

(5-10 minutes)

Isaiah 58:1-9; Luke 11:24-26
Have two different readers and a gap between the readings.

Isaiah 58:1-9a
Shout out, do not hold back!
Lift up your voice like a trumpet!
Announce to my people their rebellion,
to the house of Jacob their sins.
Yet day after day they seek me
and delight to know my ways,
as if they were a nation that practised righteousness
and did not forsake the ordinance of their God;
they ask of me righteous judgements,
they delight to draw near to God.
'Why do we fast, but you do not see?
Why humble ourselves, but you do not notice?'
Look, you serve your own interest on your fast day,
and oppress all your workers.
Look, you fast only to quarrel and to fight
and to strike with a wicked fist.
Such fasting as you do today
will not make your voice heard on high.
Is such the fast that I choose,
a day to humble oneself?

Is it to bow down the head like a bulrush,
and to lie in sackcloth and ashes?
Will you call this a fast,
a day acceptable to the Lord?
Is not this the fast that I choose:
to loose the bonds of injustice,
to undo the thongs of the yoke,
to let the oppressed go free,
and to break every yoke?
Is it not to share your bread with the hungry,
and bring the homeless poor into your house;
when you see the naked, to cover them,
and not to hide yourself from your own kin?
Then your light shall break forth like the dawn,
and your healing shall spring up quickly;
your vindicator shall go before you,
the glory of the Lord shall be your rear guard.
Then you shall call, and the Lord will answer;
you shall cry for help, and he will say, Here I am.

Luke 11:24-26

'When the unclean spirit has gone out of a person, it wanders through waterless regions looking for a resting place, but not finding any, it says, "I will return to my house from which I came." When it comes, it finds it swept and put in order. Then it goes and brings seven other spirits more evil than itself, and they enter and live there; and the last state of that person is worse than the first.'

RUMINATE

(in silence for 10-15 minutes)

See these people who parade their religion, who are self-righteous, who show off their sacrifices. These people cheat, rob, are violent and quarrelsome. Do they think they can buy God off, or that sacrifices are an alternative? Sadly, there are still people like this.

They want God to change things, but they do not want to change themselves. God wants our presence more than our presents and wants us to desire His presence more than His presents.

Why keep Lent? Is it just to deprive us of a few pleasures? Too often as Christians we give the impression that our God is one who likes to restrict and diminish us. For many people, religion is summarised as a list of 'do not's. Some think our faith is in the Ten Commandments and not in our God. Do we keep Lent to be self-righteous, or does it have a more positive meaning? Throughout history, prophets have had to speak out against fasting that was to no good purpose. Hosea, for example, speaks for God: 'I desire steadfast love and not sacrifice, the knowledge of God rather than burnt-offerings.' *(Hosea 6:6)*

Fasting can be good, especially in a consumer society. We should take note of what we consume, and what effect it has on others and on the earth. Most of us belong to a world where our appetites are over-stimulated, not only for food but for possessions, sounds and excitement. We suffer from overloading our bodies, our minds and our hearts. Our hearts were made for the eternal and no amount of filling them with things will ever satisfy us. We need to give more attention to how we eat, how we listen, how we see, and to know what effect it is all having on the poor and needy. Lent is a time to learn to see with the heart, to extend our vision. Here is some guidance from Confucius, the Chinese philosopher (551-479 BC):

> The best person is careful in these things:
> his eyes, so that they may observe;
> his ears, so that he may learn;
> his face, so that he may reflect kindness;
> his manners, so that he may show respect for other people;
> his words, so that they may be true.

This would make a good Lent rule or resolution, and it would certainly extend you. Devise a rule for the forty days of Lent and make sure it's one that brings you closer to God and to others. Lent is a time for change: a change of direction, a change of attitude, and a change of heart.

Lent can be a time when we are enriched by having less rather than more. I am always sorry for the rich young man who seemed to have it all, but who turned sorrowfully away from Jesus because he had great riches (you may like to read Matthew 19:16-22). We may have to travel light, and to slim down our needs if we are to walk the way of the Lord. It is worth every bit of the venture. Who is foolish enough to cling to perishable possessions when they are offered the treasures of the kingdom? Who would not exchange the transient for the eternal? Here are some cautionary words from St Basil:

> Do not limit the benefit of fasting merely to abstinence from food, for a true fast means refraining from evil. Loose every unjust bond, put away your resentment against your neighbour, forgive him his offences. Do not let your fast lead only to wrangling and strife. You do not eat meat, but you devour your brother; you abstain from wine, but not from insults. So all the labour of your fast is useless.

Picture a 'haunted house'. See it being cleaned out, tidied up, given a coat of paint and prepared for occupation. It looks nice, but it is empty. Nature abhors a vacuum. Soon it is occupied. See who comes – birds down the chimney and in through the windows, vagrants and squatters. Windows and doors get broken. Inside it gets worse and worse. It becomes horrible. What a waste! What a pity it never had a caring tenant.

Who or what occupies our hearts and our lives? We learn from the parable that we can drive out evil from our lives, but that it will return if we leave them empty. I am always worried for the people who seek to empty their minds in meditation, for soon they are beset by evil. To empty the mind is like trying to empty a pond. After a while you will bring up sludge and dirt. St Paul knew this and advised people to 'keep filling their minds with good things'. The only way to triumph over degenerate thoughts is to replace them with good ones. Our lives need to be occupied or they will be taken over in the same way that a neglected garden is taken over by weeds. If you only do things that require no effort, you will be overrun in no time by weeds. Yet there are many vacuous people. Many people today have dispensed with the wisdom of the past only to be full of junk and a feeling of being lost. Think of the words in the Beatles' song, 'Nowhere Man'.

We need to be filled with something. We need someone or something to fill our hearts, our minds and our spirits. This is why St Augustine wrote, 'Lord, our hearts are restless until they rest in you.'

RESPOND

(in two sections: 20 minutes group session, then 2 minutes silence, leading into the next section)

Here is a poem by Robert Herrick, an Anglican parish priest and poet (1591-1674), which your group leader might like to use to introduce this session:

Is this a Fast, to keep
the larder leane?
and cleane
from fat of Veales and Sheep?

Is it to quit the dish
of Flesh, yet still
to fill
the platter high with fish?

Is it to fast an houre
or rag'd go,
or show
a down cast look, and sour?

No: 'tis a fast, to dole
thy sheaf of wheat
and meat
unto the hungry soule.

It is to fast from strife,
from old debate
and hate:
to circumcise thy life.

To shew a heart grief-rent;
to starve thy sin,
not Bin
and that's to keep thy Lent.

Talk about the benefits of fasting, especially in a consumer society. If we are going to give something up, there must be reasons why and we must expect results. Members of the group might like to talk about the positive side of their Lent rules. Will our rules include prayer and a deepening of our relationship with God? Will they reflect our care for others, perhaps include some alms-giving or charitable work?

Look at any newspaper articles that have been brought by others in the group, or talk about vacuous living. An empty life is a wasted life, but so is a life full of rubbish. How do we ensure that we have something of the eternal reflected in our lives? Look at positive ways of living which we could embrace.

In the short silence, look at your own way of living or your Lent rule. Then place yourself in the presence, peace and power of God.

REST AND REJOICE

(continue the silence for another 3-5 minutes; final prayers, music and blessing, 5-10 minutes)

Continue to rejoice in the presence of God. Enjoy this time as a time of peace and love.

Lord, make me an instrument of your peace.
Where there is hatred, let me sow love;
where there is injury, pardon;
where there is discord, harmony;

where there is doubt, faith;
where there is despair, hope;
where there is darkness, light, and
where there is sadness, joy.
Oh Divine Master, grant that I may not
so much seek to be consoled as to console;
to be understood as to understand;
to be loved as to love;
for it is in giving that we receive;
it is in pardoning that we are pardoned;
and it is in dying that we are born to Eternal Life.

(St Francis of Assisi)

Hymn

When I needed a neighbour were you there?
Or: Christ is the world in which we move

The Blessing

God be your joy and strength;
God be your light and guide;
God be your hope and peace;
God be with you today and for ever.

Recollect

I desire steadfast love and not sacrifice, the knowledge of God
rather than burnt offerings. *(Hosea 6:6)*

Pray daily

Create in me a clean heart, O God,
and put a new and right spirit within me. *(Psalm 51:10)*

WEEK 2

Fruit Growing

Resources

Bring images of growth, not only of fields and flowers but also of people. Bring something or tell of something that is a symbol of growth in your own life of faith.

REALISE

(10 minutes)

Hymn

Will you come and follow me if I call your name?
Or: Lord, thy word abideth
Or: Father of mercies, in thy word

After the music, keep a short time of silence and affirm that you are in the presence of God. Know that he loves you and gives you himself. Seek to be aware of the reality of God in your life. To live without regard to him is to live a lie.

> Eternal light, shine in our hearts.
> Eternal goodness, deliver us from evil.
> Eternal power, be our support.
> Eternal wisdom, scatter the darkness of our ignorance.
> Eternal pity, have mercy upon us:
> that with all our heart and might and soul and strength
> we may seek your face
> and be brought by your infinite mercy
> to your holy presence, through Jesus Christ, our Lord. Amen.
> *(Alcuin of York, 735-804)*

Lord, grant that we may hear and receive your Holy Word,
not only with our ears, but with our hearts and minds also
that we may show forth its fruit in our lives,
for the benefit of all and to the glory of your holy name.

READ

(5-10 minutes)

Mark 4:1-9 (or: Matthew 13:1-9; Luke 8:4-8)

Mark 4:1-9
Again he began to teach beside the sea. Such a very large crowd
gathered around him that he got into a boat on the sea and sat
there, while the whole crowd was beside the sea on the land.
He began to teach them many things in parables, and in his
teaching he said to them: 'Listen! A sower went out to sow. And
as he sowed, some seed fell on the path, and the birds came and
ate it up. Other seed fell on rocky ground, where it did not have
much soil, and it sprang up quickly, since it had no depth of
soil. And when the sun rose, it was scorched; and since it had no
root, it withered away. Other seed fell among thorns, and the
thorns grew up and choked it, and it yielded no grain. Other
seed fell into good soil and brought forth grain, growing up and
increasing and yielding thirty and sixty and a hundredfold.'
And he said, 'Let anyone with ears to hear listen!'

RUMINATE

(in silence 10-15 minutes)

Listen! If there is no listening or paying of attention, nothing will
be heard at all. We all choose what we want to hear. It is amazing
how deaf we can be if we do not want to hear. It is hard to give
anyone our undivided attention. Those who do not listen
carefully to others are not likely to listen to God. Remember the
parables were meant to be heard rather than studied and that they
called for an immediate response.

Parables are literally something thrown against something else, but they are more than a mere comparison. One reveals the depth of the other. The more we understand about the world the more we know about its creator. The early British Church talked of three Scriptures: the Old Testament, the New Testament and the World. It is hard to understand much of the New Testament without knowing the Old, and it is hard to understand the Old Testament without understanding the World in which we live. One of the sad things about modern education is that it teaches people to read books, but it leaves them illiterate when it comes to 'reading the world'. We should heed the words of St Paul in Romans 1:20 – 'Ever since the creation of the world his eternal power and divine nature, invisible though they are, have been understood and seen through the things he has made.'

Picture the scene: the day is bright and they are by the Sea of Galilee. A large crowd has gathered to hear Jesus. The crowd is so large that he gets into a boat on the lake and speaks to them from there. The shore makes a good amphitheatre. Jesus seeks to hold their attention. Perhaps at that very moment a farmer is sowing seed on the hillside behind them. The scene would be familiar to all of them.

The sower scatters his seed; every bit of his land is meant to have some seed. Already the birds are watching and waiting. They will devour the seed that falls on the path. It will bear no fruit. Then some will fall on shallow ground. Much of the land around Jesus and his followers was like this with limestone near the surface. It will grow for a while, often growing more quickly than the rest at first, but then it will wither. The shallowness of the soil prevents growth. It will bear no fruit. More seed will be lost to thorns and thistles, which surround it, sapping its strength and choking it. Again, this seed will bear no fruit. So much is lost, wasted – is it worthwhile? Look to the harvest. See the full field. Some bore fruit, thirty, sixty, a hundredfold. Jesus then says, 'Let anyone with ears to hear listen!' If you were in the crowd, what would your reaction be? Is this only a lesson in agriculture, or something more?

This is not a story about different seeds but about different soils. There is only one soil that is truly receptive and fruit-bearing. We have to ask ourselves if we are like that soil. No doubt, Jesus often watched a sower at work. The seed was spread over the land indiscriminately, and all parts received it. Maybe he saw his own work in a similar vein and his success rate was no better than the farmer's! Not everyone is a good listener or is responsive. The fruitfulness of good soil makes it all worthwhile. If the seed is to prosper, it must be allowed entry, it must be given some depth and provided with space to grow. The seed must get in, get down, and have space to grow. How does this speak to us?

Then the seed must bear fruit. Fruit-bearing is not instant, it is often a slow process. The land needs to be prepared, nourished and weeded if fruit is to have a chance. It is no use asking which soil you are, for you are all of them. It is better to look at which areas of your life are fruitful and to develop them, or to look to see where weeding and nourishment are needed.

We hear so many words that it is hard for the Word to get into our lives at all. We live in a world of multi-choice, and so there is a danger that we may never make a lasting choice at all. We have increased our ability to communicate with each other, but have trivialised nearly all that we say. We switch on the television, or some music, but we neither watch nor listen. We are no longer good at giving our undivided attention, of truly listening to each other. We are too occupied. The sign we put up can often read, 'No room at the inn'. The Word will find no entry here. So many people have a bad habit of not listening to others. We so easily turn a deaf ear to the calls upon us. If we taught ourselves to be more attentive and receptive, how greatly our lives would be enriched.

Like seed, the Word needs some depth in order to grow to maturity within us. However, most people are always on the move; they never stay with anything for very long. People crave excitement and thrills, yet they miss the thrill of being fully receptive and alive. So much of what we do is shallow and fleeting; it may look good on the surface, or at the time, but it has no lasting power.

Much of the world is restless and cannot stay with anything for long. We fill our time and our lives with things until there is little space left. We are preoccupied, so the chance of new growth is greatly limited. Notice in Mark 4:19 how it is the cares of the world, the lure of wealth, and the desire for other things which come in and choke off growth.

Thank God for good growth and for a fertile world. Remember, it is by your fruits that you will be known (Matthew 7:20).

RESPOND

(in two sections: 20 minutes group session, then 2 minutes silence, leading into the next section)

Begin with the game 'Chinese Whispers'. Get into a circle and then whisper a sentence to the person next to you. Let this sentence be passed around until it comes back to where it started from, and see how much it has changed. Usually, the larger the group, the greater are the changes to the words. Pick a sentence that is not all that easy to pass on, one with the odd difficult word in it. Try to speak clearly, but do not repeat the sentence once you have said it. This will tell us a little about our ability to hear what is said. Now have someone read Mark 4:10-20.

Look at the symbols of growth and fruitfulness which members of the group have brought. Do we see them as full of promise? Look at the symbols of growth and fruitfulness in our own lives. Talk about the things that hinder growth in our church and community, within our own lives. How can we improve our own growing in the faith and bringing forth fruit? In silence, give thanks for what we have heard and received and for what others have shared with us.

REST AND REJOICE

(continue the silence for another 3-5 minutes; final prayers, music and blessing, 5-10 minutes)

Give thanks for points of growth in your life, for individuals who have helped you to develop as a person, for teachers and preachers. Pray that you are receptive to the word and that you bring forth fruit.

Prayers

> Lord of the harvest, we call upon you,
> that we may bring forth the fruits of the Spirit.
> Let our lives produce a good crop of love, joy, peace, patience, gentleness,
> goodness, humility and self-control,
> that we may work for the wellbeing of all
> and reveal your glory in our lives.

> God be in my head, and in my understanding.
> God be in my eyes, and in my looking.
> God be in my mouth, and in my speaking.
> God be in my heart, and in my thinking.
> God be at my end, and at my departing.
> *(Sarum Book of Hours)*

Hymn

Take my life and let it be consecrated, Lord, to thee   358
Or: Jesu, grant me this, I pray
Or: Help us to help each other, Lord
Or: If we only seek peace

The Blessing

The goodness of the Father,
the grace of Christ the Son,
the guidance of the Holy Spirit,
the glory of the Three in One
is with you now and always.

Recollect

Pray with the child Samuel, 'Speak, Lord, for your servant is listening.' Seek to give your undivided attention to God in your prayers, and to the people you meet.

WEEK 3

Where Do Weeds Come From?

Resources

Bring photographs or headlines from the newspapers of areas where goodness is being crowded out or where life is degenerate. 'Evil triumphs when good people do nothing.' Bring concerns about areas where some action should be taken. Can you give an example of weeding out in your own life?

REALISE

(10 minutes)

Hymn

Come, ye thankful people, come
Or: As the deer pants for the water
Or: Lord Jesus, think on me

After the music, keep a short time of silence and affirm that you are in the presence of God. Know that he loves you and gives you himself. Seek to be aware of the reality of God in your life. To live without regard to him is to live a lie. Try to prevent your mind from wandering. Concentrate on the words, 'You, Lord, are here.' Repeat the words until you become aware of the reality that they represent.

> O God, ever with us,
> Open our eyes to your presence.
> Open our ears to your word.
> Open our lips to sing your praises.
> Open our hearts to your love.
> Let nothing take us from you

that we may know and love you
this day and for evermore.

O Lord, the help of the helpless,
the hope of the hopeless,
the Saviour of the storm-tossed,
the harbour of voyagers,
the physician of the sick,
we pray to you.
O Lord, you know each of us, and our petitions,
you know each house and its needs,
receive us all into your kingdom;
make us children of light,
and bestow your peace and love upon us.

(Basil of Caesarea, 330-379)

READ

(5-10 minutes) Matthew 13:24-30, 36-43 (Let there be a reader for each section.)

Matthew 13:24-30

He put before them another parable: 'The kingdom of heaven may be compared to someone who sowed good seed in his field; but while everybody was asleep, an enemy came and sowed weeds among the wheat, and then went away. So when the plants came up and bore grain, then the weeds appeared as well. And the slaves of the householder came and said to him, "Master, did you not sow good seed in your field? Where, then, did these weeds come from?" He answered, "An enemy has done this." The slaves said to him, "Then do you want us to go and gather them?" But he replied, "No; for in gathering the weeds you would uproot the wheat along with them. Let both of them grow together until the harvest; and at harvest time I will tell the reapers, Collect the weeds first and bind them in bundles to be burned, but gather the wheat into my barn."'

Matthew 13:36-43
Then he left the crowds and went into the house. And his disciples approached him, saying, 'explain to us the parable of the weeds of the field.' He answered, 'The one who sows the good seed is the Son of Man; the field is the world, and the good seed are the children of the kingdom; the weeds are the children of the evil one, and the enemy who sowed them is the devil; the harvest is the end of the age, and the reapers are angels. Just as the weeds are collected and burned up with fire, so will it be at the end of the age. The Son of Man will send his angels, and they will collect out of his kingdom all causes of sin and all evil-doers, and they will throw them into the furnace of fire, where there will be weeping and gnashing of teeth. Then the righteous will shine like the sun in the kingdom of their Father. Let anyone with ears listen!'

RUMINATE

(in silence 10-15 minutes)

Here is another scene which Jesus' listeners would well understand. I feel a deep sympathy with the servant who asked his master, 'Where did these weeds come from?' Many a time I have cleared my garden of weeds only to find that they have returned in no time.

The seed that was sown was good seed and it would provide a good crop. But while they were sleeping, an enemy came and sowed bad seed. Often it is in unguarded moments that evil gains entry into our lives. Someone may want to say, 'Why blame an enemy, as fields always produce weeds?' Well, there is a suggestion here that it was not always so. The weed in this story is 'tares', or 'bearded darnel', and there is a tradition that it was once good seed which had gone wrong at the time of the Fall of Adam and Eve. The Jews called it 'bastard wheat', believing it to be born out of an illicit union.

Darnel was one of the greatest problems for farmers, because of its close resemblance to wheat. It looks so much like the good crop at the early stages of its growth. By the time it is recognisable, the roots of the wheat and the darnel are intertwined, and to pull out one would destroy the other. Hence the advice, 'Let both grow until the harvest.' At harvest time, the plants will be separated by hand and the darnel burned. The darnel could not be left with the wheat, for the darnel is unpleasant to taste, and it can cause sickness and dizziness, as it is a narcotic. Fortunately, at harvest time, the plant is a dirty-grey colour and can be recognised.

It may sound absurd to us that anyone would sow bad seed in another's field, but it has been known for enemies to do this. Under Roman law, the sowing of bad seed in a field was a criminal offence and punishable. An old threat used by farmers in India was, 'I will sow bad seed in your field.'

Jesus was in no doubt that there is always a hostile element at work in this world and in us. We need to be constantly on our guard against our lives degenerating into something that is destructive to either ourselves or to others. People often tell me that they like to do what comes naturally. My response to this is, look at a garden that is let grow naturally: it will soon produce many weeds and less flowers or vegetables. If you want a good garden, you have to work at it. I have also learned that it is no use weeding and then leaving a garden empty, for the weeds will soon return. Empty spaces, and, in the same way, empty lives, soon get overrun. To keep the garden from being overrun, it is necessary to fill it with good things. It is the same laws which are at work where we're concerned.

We should never underestimate the powers of evil or be deceived by looks. Leading out of Keswick, with beautiful views of Lake Derwentwater, is the road to Watendlath. All around it, the scenery is breathtaking. Beauty fills the eye on this road, which goes on to Borrowdale. It was on this road that Rogue Herries met a wandering country preacher called Robert Finch.

> Herries asked: 'How shall I like this place? It is cut off from the world.' There was an odd note of scorn in the little man's voice as he answered. 'It is the world, sir. Here within these hills, in this space of ground, is all the world. I thought that while I was with

35

Lord Petersham all the world was there, but in every village through which I have passed since then I have found the whole world – all anger and vanity and covetousness and lust, yes, and all charity, goodness and sweetness of soul. But most of all here in this valley, I have found the whole world . . . You will find everything here, sir. God and the devil both walk in these fields.'
Rogue Herries, Hugh Walpole

Both 'God and the devil walk in these fields' is a notice that could be put up on any place of beauty, or on any individual. No life or place is free from the danger of degeneration or evil, no matter how sanctified. I used to tell people I lived in one of the holiest places in England, on Holy Island, sanctified by the saints and prayer. I had the key to the church. I was able to enter this special place and have it to myself. I once knelt down near where St Aidan used to pray, and then thought the wickedest thoughts of the week! As I am human, this happens to me, and I had to weed out these thoughts and replace them with others. Perhaps, long before I was there, St Aidan had once wrestled in the same way. We need to be constantly on our guard and to replace any evil with good.

It is not always that easy to tell which are weeds. Recently, a friend of mine did some weeding for me and I lost many of the flowers I had been nurturing. Another friend said to me, 'It is easy to recognise weeds. Pull everything out of your garden. If it comes back, it's a weed!' This is not a policy I would recommend: it is not always easy to sort out the good from the bad. Too much can be destroyed by hasty decisions. We should be careful about labelling people or making swift judgements. Just as there is in a field, there is always potential for change in people. Yet, we have to remember that there is a harvest, that there is a time when seeds will be seen for what they are. There is a time when judgements and separations will be made.

RESPOND

(in two sections: 20 minutes group session, then 2 minutes silence, leading into the next section)

What is your immediate reaction? Every life is like the field sown with good and bad seed. We are not a weed-free field. There is some weeding that is good and necessary, yet at times we need to be very careful. It is no use pulling out weeds if we do not then fill the space. Remember the parable of the 'Haunted House'.

Look at the photographs and cuttings that have been brought to the group session. Sometimes, it is too easy to condemn. The image which people often have of the Church is one in which it is against the pleasures of life. We need look at the sort of people Jesus chose to follow him. They were far from perfect. Often Jesus looked at the potential rather than the present situation. Someone like Matthew would never have been called if Jesus were looking for people with perfect lives. Jesus calls us from where we are, but he does seek obedience and he says, 'Sin no more'. I love to see a newly ploughed field, but I know that it mustn't stay empty: it needs to produce a crop. In the same way, I do not like to see fields that have been set aside and are barren of life. The land and humans are meant to produce fruit. 'By their fruits you shall know them.' *(Matthew 7:16)*

How can we improve the community and area in which we live? A friend describes weeds as 'flowers in the wrong place'. Can we improve our area so that it makes people feel at ease and at home? How do you go about changing your own life? How do you weed out the things that spoil good crops? You might like to think about the dangers of what we take into our lives by watching films which are violent or which exploit sex. How do you guard against greed, anger or bitterness?

The mind is like a tape recorder, and it records all that you ever watch, see or experience. When we are tired, this tape recorder tends to play at random and our thoughts bring out all sorts of weeds. The more good you put on the tape, the more likely it is that good will appear when we are tired. Read Philippians 4:4-9. Think about this in the silence that follows.

REST AND REJOICE

(continue the silence for another 3-5 minutes; final prayers, music and blessing, 5-10 minutes)

Rejoice in the presence of God. Affirm again, 'You, Lord, are here.' Let these words stop your mind from wandering. Use them as an anchor. Every time you drift away, let these words haul you back. As time goes on, I like to shorten the sentence bit by bit:

'You, Lord, are here.'
'You, Lord, are.'
'You, Lord.'
'You.'

So, rest and rejoice in the peace, power and presence of God. Use this sentence throughout the week to check all wandering thoughts. Remember, you are not trying to make something happen, but rather to awaken yourself to the reality of God's presence and peace.

Prayers

Here is my heart, O God,
here it is with all its secrets;
look into my thoughts,
O my hope,
and take away all my wrong feelings.
Let my eyes be ever on you
and release my feet from the snare.
(*St Augustine*, Confessions IV:6)

Peace, Lord, be in my heart and mind
Peace, Lord, in my actions and in my dealings
Peace, Lord, in my home and in all relationships
Peace, Lord, in each community and in the world
Peace, Lord, the deep, deep peace of God be upon us
Peace, Lord, be within us and with us always.

Hymn

O Jesus I have promised
Or: O for a heart to praise my God
Or: Give me joy in my heart

The Blessing

God, in his holiness, protect you,
Christ, in his majesty, save you,
the Holy Spirit, on high, inspire you,
that your life may be full of peace and love.
And the blessing of God Almighty, the Father,
the Son and the Holy Spirit be upon you now and evermore.

Recollect

'If there is any excellence and if there is anything worthy of praise, think about these things' (Philippians 4:8). At every opportunity seek to bring good things to mind and rejoice in the presence of God. Say as often as possible, 'You, Lord, are here.'

WEEK 4

The Dangers of Jerry-Builders

Resources
Bring things which illustrate bad planning or building on bad
foundations. Photographs of crumbling buildings might give you
the courage to talk about bits of your life which need a firmer base
to build on. Re-look at your Lent resolution.

REALISE
(10 minutes)

Hymn
Be Thou my vision, O Lord of my heart
Or: The wise man built his house upon the rock
Or: All my hope on God is founded
Or: Will your anchor hold in the storms of life?

After the music, keep a short time of silence and affirm that you
are in the presence of God. Know that he loves you and gives you
himself. Seek to be aware of the reality of God in your life. To live
without regard to him is to live a lie.

> Do not be afraid to throw yourself on the Lord!
> He will not draw back and let you fall!
> Put your worries aside and throw yourself on him:
> he will welcome and heal you.
> (St Augustine, Confessions VIII:11)

Give us grace, O Lord,
not only to hear your word with our ears,
but also to receive it into our hearts
and to show it forth in our lives;
for the glory of thy great name.
(Source unknown)

My dearest Lord,
be a bright flame before me:
be a guiding star above me:
be a smooth path beneath me:
be a kindly Shepherd behind me:
today, tonight and for ever.
(Attributed to St Columba)

READ

(5-10 minutes)

Matthew 7:24-27 (or: Luke 6:47-49)

Matthew 7:24-27
'Everyone then who hears these words of mine and acts on
them will be like a wise man who built his house on rock. The
rain fell, the floods came, and the winds blew and beat on that
house, but it did not fall, because it had been founded on rock.
And everyone who hears these words of mine and does not act
on them will be like a foolish man who built his house on sand.
The rain fell, and the floods came, and the winds blew and beat
against that house, and it fell – and great was its fall!'

RUMINATE

(in silence 10-15 minutes)

Jesus would have been brought up to know the Scriptures,
perhaps he had heard someone preaching upon Proverbs 10:25.

'When the tempest passes, the wicked are no more, but the righteous are established for ever.' The grammar school I went to had a Latin inscription engraved in stone by the entrance to the building. Slowly, I would learn the importance of the words from Psalm 127:1, 'Unless the Lord builds the house, those who build it labour in vain.' Foundations are important even if they are hidden.

When you listen to the story of the two builders, there is a hint of Jesus' humour. Jesus must have caused some laughter when he described the man who built in what was a riverbed. Who would build his house in a 'wadi'? Sadly, it is possible, and some people can be ever so foolish. In the summer, a wadi can look like a pleasant sandy hollow – it is only when the storms come that it becomes a raging river.

So there are two men, one in a hurry to build his house, the other determined to build his house properly. The first man quickly chooses a place without giving much thought to the future. He wants to get going, speed is of the essence. Foundations, he thinks, are something that no one sees, so why spend so much time on them? Everything this man will build is on a shallow base. Most likely, he would not have dug down to rock, even if he were not building in a wadi. You can imagine him mocking the slowness of his neighbour. He will be in his house first and living comfortably before his neighbour has done much building. He builds for show and outward appearance, but he is exchanging his future for an easy time now.

The second man spends a lot of time just getting down to the rock. He is determined that his house will have a firm base. While he makes steady progress, his near neighbour's house goes up fast – he fears he might not be finished before the winter rains, but the first man is sitting back and enjoying himself.

Then the rains come. For a while, both men have good shelter; each has a covering over his head. Then the river begins to rise. The house on the rock does not shake in the storm, because it is on a firm foundation. The other house, however, begins to quiver and shake and so does its occupant. Floods overwhelm it. Water destroys it. It falls, and 'great was its fall'.

I heard once of a kindly builder. He asked a man, who had worked for him for a long time, to build a house while he was away. The man decided this was a time to take it easy. He didn't bother very much with the foundations. He bought cheap materials and pocketed some of the money. He took on a few jerry-builders and let them loose on the house. Throughout the building of the house he used inferior products. When cracks appeared, he plastered or painted over them. On the surface, it looked all right, but it was a poor building. Such a building would give endless problems in the future. When the builder returned, he met the man and said, 'Here are the keys. I did not want you to know until I returned. This house is yours!'

It is easy to miss the beginning of this story from Jesus: 'Everyone who hears these words of mine and acts upon them is like a wise man.' This parable is about listening and obeying. In our world of a multitude of sounds, we all choose what we want to hear. We tune our ears, our radios, televisions and lives to receive only certain things. In our desire for speed, we often rush or switch from one thing to another and never stay with anything for long. In a consumer society such as our own, little is savoured and often quantity has replaced quality. In all of this, what happens to our relationship with our God and the way we receive his Word? For much of the world, worship is seen as a leisure pursuit and only one option among many. In the busy life we live the Word of God is often crowded out or given very little attention. God is not an extra option!

Hearing is not enough, however. True hearing demands not only undivided attention, but also a reaction. When the Scriptures talk of hearing, they mean 'hearing and obeying'. To know the words is not sufficient in itself. The devil himself knows the words! I know someone who has studied theology, but who is an atheist. True theology is not the ability to pass an exam or to have a degree in Divinity, it is rather the way we live.

Listening is of basic importance. I believe that anyone who does not listen carefully to other people will not listen to God. In true listening, we learn to give ourselves without distraction. If we do not hear properly, we will not react properly. Listening is the beginning of the giving of ourself without stint, to another. If we do not listen with full attention to the Word of God, we are not likely to obey it. I learned to sing in Sunday School:

When we walk with the Lord
in the light of his word
what glory he sheds on our way!
While we do his good will,
he abides with us still,
and with all who will trust and obey.

Trust and obey.
There's no other way,
to be happy in Jesus,
but to trust and obey.

At this point in St Matthew's Gospel, we move on from Jesus' teaching to his deeds. Good hearing is shown by our actions.

RESPOND

(in two sections: 20 minutes group session, then 2 minutes silence, leading into the next section)

You may like to begin this session with another game of 'Chinese Whispers'. Once again, it tells us about how we listen.

How well do you listen to the readings of Scripture? Very often in church, I find that after the service few people can tell me what the readings were. We have learned to ignore words because of all the sounds about us. Try, for a week, to not put the radio or television on unless there is something you really want to hear. Allow some silence in your life. Often God speaks with a 'still small voice'. I learned at college that 'God speaks most to those who can keep silence'. Jesus knew that one of the greatest impediments to the Word, is people who do not listen.

At the beginning of the twentieth century, great cracks appeared in Winchester Cathedral. Something had to be done before the cathedral collapsed. It was suggested that great buttresses should be built to shore up the building. Other suggestions were to tie bars from wall to wall, that great favourite of the Victorians. One man insisted that they looked for the cause of the trouble, and not at the symptoms. It was discovered that the fault lay with the foundations. The cathedral had been built on a peat bog. Over the centuries, and with better drainage in the city, the peat bog had dried out and shrunk. The cathedral had great spaces between it and the peat in many areas. Over five-and-a-half years, concrete blocks were brought in to replace the peat. This was a difficult process, but it was necessary for the cathedral to be on a firm foundation.

Look at any photographs that have been brought to the session. What causes buildings and societies to crumble? What is the cure for some of the situations we are looking at? How good are we at listening to each other and how can we improve this?

In the quiet, look at your Lent resolution; see if you want to revise it or add to it.

REST AND REJOICE

(continue the silence for another 3-5 minutes; final prayers, music and blessing, 5-10 minutes)

Rejoice in the presence, the peace, and the power of God.
Read Isaiah 43:1-7 and think upon the reality of these words.

Prayers

O Almighty God, who alone can order the unruly wills and affections of sinful people: grant to your people, that they may love the thing which you command and desire that which you do promise; that so, among the sundry and manifold changes of the world, our hearts may surely there be fixed, where true joys are to be found; through Jesus Christ our Lord. Amen.

(Collect for the Fourth Sunday after Easter,
adapted from the Book of Common Prayer)

Lord, give me
a quiet heart, that I may hear you:
a generous heart, that I may receive you:
an obedient heart, that I may serve you:
a pure heart, that I may see you:
a loving heart, that I may abide in you
this day and for ever.

Hymn

Christ is made the sure foundation
Or: When I walk with the Lord
Or: Do not be afraid, for I have redeemed you
Or: Glorious things of Thee are spoken

The Blessing

The love of the Father enfold you.
The love of the Saviour uphold you.
The love of the Spirit surround you.
May you find in God a sure foundation:
and the blessing of the Almighty
be upon you now and for ever.

Recollect

Seek to be attentive to others this week. Learn again to listen with full attention. Tune in daily to the reality of God's presence and say often: 'God is my strength and my salvation, a very present help in trouble.'

WEEK 5
Use it or Lose it

Resources

Bring photographs of talented people or people using their talents. Remember that we are all talented, and so don't just bring shots of pop idols. Bring something that reveals a talent of your own – a piece of music, a poem, a painting, even a duster! Something that is a sign of what you are good at. Art materials could be used to make a collage or a frieze, showing the talents of the group. Some could be given flowers to help to beautify the room with a floral display. Everyone could be given a talent (e.g. a £1 coin) to take home with the idea that they will make it grow and return with the growth.

REALISE

(10 minutes)

Hymn

Lord of all hopefulness
Or: Father, we adore you
Or: Take my life and let it be

After the music keep a short time of silence and affirm that you are in the presence of God. Know that he loves you and gives you himself. Seek to be aware of the reality of God in your life. To live without regard to him is to live a lie.

We place ourselves:
in the presence of the Father, who created us *out* of love and *for* his love;
in the presence of the Son, who redeemed us *by* his love and *for* his love;
in the presence of the Spirit, who sustains us *by* his love and *for* his love.

Confess

Creator God, forgive our lack of vision.
We have failed to acknowledge the world belongs to you.
We have not cared enough about the wellbeing of the world.
We have often wasted our talents and time and brought little to
full growth.
We have not had enough respect for our neighbours or ourselves.
We have used words and actions that are not worthy of
co-creators.
Lord, forgive us, heal us, redeem us and sustain us.

Leader

Almighty God, have mercy upon us, forgive us our sins, confirm and strengthen us in all goodness, and continue to give us a share in creation, through Jesus Christ our Saviour, who lives and reigns with you and the Holy Spirit now and forever.

For the magnificence of the universe
God of all, **we praise you**.
For the majesty of the earth
God of all, **we praise you**.
For the talents you have given us
God of all, **we praise you**.
For all that we have achieved
God of all, **we praise you**.
For your power within all things
God of all, **we praise you**.

7.40

READ

(5-10 minutes)

Matthew 25:14-30

'For it is as if a man, going on a journey, summoned his slaves and entrusted his property to them; to one he gave five talents, to another two, to another one, to each according to his ability. Then he went away. The one who had received the five talents went off at once and traded with them, and made five more talents. In the same way, the one who had the two talents made two more talents. But the one who had received the one talent went off and dug a hole in the ground and hid his master's money. After a long time the master of those slaves came and settled accounts with them. Then the one who had received the five talents came forward, bringing five more talents, saying "Master, you handed over to me five talents; see, I have made five more talents." His master said to him, "Well done, good and trustworthy slave; you have been trustworthy in a few things, I will put you in charge of many things; enter into the joy of your master." And the one with the two talents also came forward, saying, "Master, you handed over to me two talents; see, I have made two more talents." His master said to him, "Well done, good and trustworthy slave; you have been trustworthy in a few things, I will put you in charge of many things; enter into the joy of your master." Then the one who had received the one talent also came forward, saying, "Master, I knew that you were a harsh man, reaping where you did not sow, and gathering where you did not scatter seed; so I was afraid, and I went and hid your talent in the ground. Here you have what is yours." But his master replied, "You wicked and lazy slave! You knew, did you, that I reap where I did not sow, and gather where I did not scatter? Then you ought to have invested my money with the bankers, and on my return I would have received what was my own with interest. So take the talent from him, and give it to the one with the ten talents. For to all those who have, more will be given, and they will have an abundance; but from those who have nothing, even what they have will be taken away. As for this worthless slave, throw him into the outer darkness, where there will be weeping and gnashing of teeth." '

You may like to use the following sketch to help people see the parable:

The Talent for Adventure and Growth

Narrator
Once upon a time, the owner of a large estate went away, leaving it in the hands of the tenants. He loved and trusted them and gave each of them enough to work with. He gave with great generosity, to one £500,000, to another £250,000, and to another £100,000. Each person had plenty for their wellbeing and growth.

First person
'What would you do with half a million? Go on a cruise, throw a great party or start a business? I took it and bought raw material, wood that had never been worked, silver that had never been shaped, gold that nobody had worked on.'

Narrator
In shaping them, he shaped himself: he used his talent and it developed. He grew with his business and so did his bank balance. He became a good craftsman, more skilled and gifted. It had been a big risk, but it paid off. He was on his way to making a fortune and to becoming a more creative person himself.

Second person
'What would you do with quarter of a million? It would be very nice to play with, I mean work with. It would bring in a good bit if invested. I have always loved the earth, so I bought a piece of land. I worked the land. I bought seeds, dealing in potentials rather than actualities. You have to have faith in the future to plant.

I worked long and hard and at first there were not many signs of returns. For a while, all the money was gone and there was little to show for it. It was a risky business. Then suddenly the growth was wonderful; it was exciting to share in creation.'

Narrator

With the developing of the land, she developed. She gained wisdom as well as trust. She grew as the land progressed, she matured with the crops, and her money, too, started to grow with the crops. Her confidence and her joy grew. All were maturing together.

Third person

'What a lot of money I have got. What a lot of responsibility! I shall have to put a lot of thought into what I do. I must be careful and not do anything risky. While I sat back and thought, I buried the money; no one could see it, no one could use it. There is no doubt I like work, I sit and think about it for hours!'

Narrator

He was a sad creature, too afraid to live. He was not an adventurer. He was not a risk-taker. He was afraid to lose anything, and he was not sure of the owner of the estate. He was afraid to move. If you bury seed, it grows, but if you bury talent, it dies.

Suddenly the generous master returned, as they knew he would. It was Accounts Day. Out came the book of reckoning. A man came with a group of wonderful sculptures, statues and engravings. In shaping them, he had shaped himself. In enriching the raw materials, he had grown and also been enriched. He was a fuller and a better person than before.

Owner

'Well done, good and faithful servant. Because I can trust you here, I can trust you anywhere.'

Narrator
Then a farmer appeared. She did not really feel comfortable here. She would rather be out in the fields, sharing in creation. She had little to show: the fresh seed had been planted, but it was hardly showing. The crop had been sold and the proceeds put back into the land. The creative owner could see what was done and was delighted – here was a co-creator.

Owner
'Well done, good and faithful servant. Because I can trust you here, I can trust you anywhere.'

Narrator
In came the next man with a big bag of money. He hadn't lost a penny. He hadn't made a penny. He hadn't risked anything. It had been buried, but it was all there. He could account for every penny. He hadn't thought of putting it to work for him. He hadn't thought of it giving him the chance to grow. He hadn't invested it. He hadn't shaped himself. In fact, in every way, he just 'hadn't'. He'd buried his talents and abilities and they had diminished and died. In doing so, he'd lost touch with his creator and with himself. He'd lost his creative spirit. He was a good man, but, sadly, good for nothing!

Owner
The owner and creator of the estate was heard to say: 'Did they not know I was measuring them far more than the things they collected? I am saddened by anyone who does not grow; it is a waste of talent and a life. Someone else may as well have your talent if you do not use it.'

RUMINATE
(in silence 10-15 minutes)

The whole of Matthew 25 is about Judgement, about those who are ill-prepared, those who waste their gifts, and about insensitivity in relationships with others. All of this chapter could give us much food for thought.

In the parable of the talents, the message is simple: 'use it or lose it'. Think for a few moments of what we have lost through not using our talents properly. Living in the country, I hear people complain about the loss of the local shop and the butcher, but they actually shopped at the supermarket. They bemoan the loss of the local bus, but they always travelled by car. The message, then, is: use it or lose it. The same is true of the ability to play music well, or to dance well – use it or lose it. It is not the amount of talent that matters, it is how we use it. Small talents grow with use. Modern research has shown that nearly everyone has far greater potential that they ever use. How much better we would feel, how much more enriched the world would be, if only we would risk a little to increase our potential.

The emphasis in the story is on the wasted talent. A talent was a weight, not an amount of money. The value of the talent depended on what it was made of. Talents were usually made of gold, silver or copper. The commonest were of silver. Perhaps the one who received the least just did not want this new gift to disturb his way of life. For some, any change in life is threatening, and this says something about our faith.

The Scribes and Pharisees resisted any change. They sought to build a fence around the law. Change was forbidden. We see this sort of reaction by Saint Peter in Acts 10: Peter's reply to God, when he was asked to do something new, was: 'Certainly not, Lord, I have never.'(Verse 14). This reminds me of the rhyme:

Our family have been churchwardens
for a thousand years or so
and to every question
we have always answered, 'No!'

So much is lost by the unwillingness to take a risk or to be adventurous. For many, religion is something negative: people justify themselves not by their actions, but by what they have not done. The condemnation is not that we have been wicked, but that we haven't been anything at all. A New Testament Greek word which describes sin can be translated as 'missing the mark', living 'below par', and that is a greater danger for most than any wickedness. Negativity, or apathy, is good for nothing. Remember, Jesus came that we should have life and life in all its fullness.

At baptisms, I have often offered to give the parents a cheque for £10,000. I tell them: 'Frame it! Don't use it!' This is what we tend to do to many of the gifts that God gives us. The message of the parable is clear: 'use it or lose it'.

Notice that the man in the Gospel story said, 'I was afraid.' This is not a good basis for a relationship with our God. Our faith is built on love, not on fear. I am told there are 365 texts in the Scriptures that say, 'Fear not' or: 'Do not be afraid'. We should take these texts to heart. If you would like to think upon a text saying 'Do not be afraid', read Isaiah 43:1-3.

RESPOND

(in two sections: 20 minutes group session, then 2 minutes silence, leading into the next section)

Look at the photographs of people with talents. How do they achieve what they do? Talk about your own talents and how you hope to develop them. Remember that all of us have hidden talents which we have still not used. The Church has one of the greatest resources of human talent in the world, but sadly it often does not know how to release it. We cloister people when we should be encouraging them to be adventurous and grow. Discuss how you will increase a gift of £1, were you to be given one. In the silence think over: 'All good gifts around us are sent from heaven above; then thank the Lord, O thank the Lord, for all his love.'

REST AND REJOICE

(continue the silence for another 3-5 minutes; final prayers, music and blessing, 5-10 minutes)

Prayers

For all who share in your creative spirit
For all who are co-creators
For all who are parents, all who are caring for others
For all who work the land, all who provide us with food
Creator, hear our prayer.

For artists, musicians and craft workers
For teachers, preachers, doctors and nurses
For all who work in conservation
For those who improve and enrich our environment
Creator, hear our prayer.

For those who have lost their vocation
For all who feel their talents are wasted
For all who are restricted by poverty or oppression
For all who go unnoticed or are unappreciated
Creator, hear our prayer.

Father of all creation, we thank you that you have given us a world rich in resources, and invited us to share in your creative spirit. Help us to accept with joy the abilities you have given us, neither wasting nor misusing your creation. May we act with reverence and love towards all things and so reflect the great love you have for your creation.

God, give us grace to accept with serenity
the things that cannot be changed,
courage to change the things that should be changed,
and the wisdom to know the difference.

(Reinhold Niebuhr, 1892-1971)

55

Hymn

Lord of all power, I give you my will
Or: Fill thou my Life, O lord my God
Or: All that I am'

The Blessing

The Father guard you and each action,
the Son protect you and each thought.
The Spirit guide you in all your dealings,
and the blessing of the Giver of all good gifts
be upon you and all that you do, now and evermore.

WEEK 6
At Home

Resources

Bring photographs of your home, your family, or the community in which you live to the session. From the local paper, bring articles that show a caring community. Bring symbols of love, forgiveness and acceptance.

REALISE

(10 minutes)

Hymn

Amazing Grace
Or: Dear Lord and Father of mankind
Or: Father of heaven, whose love profound

After the music, keep a short time of silence and affirm that you are in the presence of God. Know that he loves you and gives you himself. Seek to be aware of the reality of God in your life. To live without regard to him is to live a lie.

Lord who created me, I come to you.
Lord who gave me freedom, I come to you.
Lord who allowed me to go, I come to you.
Lord who longed for my return, I come to you.
Lord who sought me, I come to you.
Lord who rescued me, I come to you.
Lord who bought me, I come to you.
Lord who rejoiced at my returning, I come to you.
Lord who accepted me, I come to you.

Lord who enriched me, I come to you.
Lord enfolding me in your love, I come to you.
Set our hearts on fire with love for you, O Christ,
that in the flame we may love you
with all our hearts,
with all our minds,
with all our souls,
and with all our strength,
and our neighbours as ourselves,
so that keeping your commandments,
we may glorify you, the giver of all good gifts.
  (Kontakion for Love, Eastern Orthodox Church)

READ

(5-10 minutes)

Luke 15:11-32
Then Jesus said, 'There was a man who had two sons. The younger of them said to his father, "Father, give me the share of the property that will belong to me." So he divided his property between them. A few days later the younger son gathered all he had and travelled to a distant country, and there he squandered his property in dissolute living. When he had spent everything, a severe famine took place throughout that country, and he began to be in need. So he went and hired himself out to one of the citizens of that country, who sent him to his fields to feed the pigs. He would gladly have filled himself with the pods that the pigs were eating; and no one gave him anything. But when he came to himself he said, "How many of my father's hired hands have bread enough and to spare, but here I am dying of hunger! I will get up and go to my father, and I will say to him, 'Father, I have sinned against heaven and before you; I am no longer worthy to be called your son; treat me like one of your hired hands.'" So he set off and went to his father. But while he was still far off, his father saw him and was filled with compassion; he ran and put

his arms around him and kissed him. Then the son said to him, "Father, I have sinned against heaven and before you; I am no longer worthy to be called your son." But the father said to his slaves, "Quickly, bring out a robe – the best one – and put it on him; put a ring on his finger and sandals on his feet. And get the fatted calf and kill it, and let us eat and celebrate; for this son of mine was dead and is alive again; he was lost and is found!" And they began to celebrate.

'Now his elder son was in the field; and when he came and approached the house, he heard music and dancing. He called one of the slaves and asked what was going on. He replied, "Your brother has come, and your father has killed the fatted calf, because he has got him back safe and sound." Then he became angry and refused to go in. His father came out and began to plead with him. But he answered his father, "Listen! For all these years I have been working like a slave for you, and I have never disobeyed your command; yet you have never given me even a young goat so that I might celebrate with my friends. But when this son of yours came back, who has devoured your property with prostitutes, you killed the fatted calf for him!" Then the father said to him, "Son, you are always with me, and all that is mine is yours. But we had to celebrate and rejoice, because this brother of yours was dead and has come to life; he was lost and has been found." '

RUMINATE

(in silence 10-15 minutes)

The whole of Luke Chapter 15 is about the lost and found. The sheep is lost through its own waywardness; the coin is lost through accident or carelessness; a son is lost through wilfulness, and another through self-righteousness. In all cases, love seeks them out. If you have ever lost anything that you love, I am sure that the time you have spent trying to find it will have exceeded its actual monetary value. If you care for it, you won't just forget it or replace it with something else. You will look for it until you find it.

The story of the two sons is in danger of missing the point if we concentrate just on one son. This is a story of a father, his children and their relationships. The story has four scenes:

Scene 1 – If this is home, I am sick of it

Scene 2 – Homesickness

Scene 3 – Home

Scene 4 – Not at home

The first scene is a common experience for much of humanity. Young adults want to stretch their wings. They want to become independent. Teenagers can be a great trial to their parents! Yet all parents know they will have to allow their children freedom some day. It takes great wisdom to know when. Sadly, many young folk fail to realise where they are loved and well off. Often words can be hurtful. By demanding his inheritance, the young man in the story was virtually saying to his father, 'Drop dead.' Imagine the pain and the deep sorrow the father would have had as he gave his son the freedom and the wherewithal to leave. Home can often be where we are treated the best but where we act the worst. We fail to appreciate what is done for us. Here is a cautionary tale told by Rabindrath Tagore, the Indian poet and Nobel Laureate:

At midnight, the would-be ascetic announced, 'This is the time to give up my home and look for God. Ah, who has held me so long in delusion here?' God whispered, 'I', but the ears of the man were stopped. With a baby asleep at her breast lay his wife peacefully sleeping at one side of the bed. The man said, 'Who are ye that have fooled me so long?' The voice said again, 'They are God', but he heard it not. The baby cried out in a dream and nestled close to its mother. God commanded, 'Stop, fool, leave not thy home.' But still he heard it not. God sighed and complained, 'Why does my servant wander to seek me, forsaking me?' One day we will learn that God teaches us of his love through our own loved ones.

Scene 2 is in a far country. Let it be said that the far country is often one of the heart. I know people who live in close proximity to each other, but who are far apart. The son has moved from where he was loved to a place where his money tries to buy love. When the heart fails to appreciate what we have, we end up in a desert country. For many people today the desert is within: things cannot satisfy the hunger for love, they can only hide it for a while. In his poem 'The Hound of Heaven', Francis Thompson has some very strong lines concerning anyone who forsakes God:

'All things betray thee, who betrayest Me.'
'Lo! naught contents thee, who content'st not Me.'
'Thou dravest love from thee, who dravest Me.'

There is a time when we all find ourselves in a far country, where we hunger and thirst for love. Augustine said of this experience, 'Lord, our hearts are restless until they rest in you.'

The young man comes to his senses through his experiences. He is homesick. He says, 'I will arise and go to my father.' This always sounds like a resurrection experience to me. The Son knows his unworthiness, his sinfulness, but he also knows the love of the father. He is not a worthy son, yet he knows that father will accept him. So he sets off for home.

What a wonderful scene is that of the homecoming. All this time the father has been on the lookout. The father does what no Eastern father would do. He runs to meet his son. The father does not stand on his dignity. He knows that if he did not accept his wayward son no one else would. So often we will learn that if we draw near to God he is waiting to come to us. The son is accepted, unworthy though he is, with love. There is great joy in the household. The son is welcomed home, reinstated, clothed, given sandals and a ring. In our turning to God, there is always an element of homecoming. It would be enough if the play ended there. But there is a strong last scene.

The eldest brother had been hard at work. When he came up to the house, he heard the music and smelled the food. There was obviously a party going on. Something wonderful must have

61

happened. When he was told it was because his wayward brother had returned, he was furious. This wastrel, he felt, had no right to come back. The eldest brother was angry, jealous and refused to enter the house. This in itself was a great public insult to the father. The father could have compelled him by force to come in. Instead, the father went out to where he was. This son was very self-righteous; he had earned it all or so he thought. The father was certainly willing to give it all to him, but by his own grace and not by compulsion. We can never earn love, we can only learn to accept it and respond to it. The self-righteous son was very like the Scribes and Pharisees, or some in the Church today, thinking he had earned his place and that it was for him alone. The love of God and his gifts are gifts of grace and not earned by works. Some people will never learn this, and these people are never truly at home. The final words are, 'You are always with me, and all that is mine is yours. But we had to celebrate and rejoice, because this brother of yours was dead and has come to life; he was lost and has been found.' Here the curtain closes. Did the older brother ever go in, or did he stay outside? The self-righteous son is not really at home, while the returned son rejoices in the father's love and forgiveness. Where do you see yourself in this story? When the curtain comes down, where will you be?

RESPOND

(in two sections: 20 minutes group session, then 2 minutes silence, leading into the next section)

Look at the photographs of home and community. Share with each other the delights and sorrows of relationships. What are the signs that your church or community is loving, caring and accepting?

The danger with the self-righteous is that they are sure that everyone else is wrong. We can all show this attitude at times. Discuss ways of making your church more inviting and welcoming, one where people feel at home.

The story is about the grace and love of God, which we cannot earn, only accept. Talk about ways in your life you understand that grace. In the silence that follows, read over John Newton's hymn 'Amazing Grace'. See how it applies to you, then give thanks for your home and loved ones.

REST AND REJOICE

(continue the silence for another 3-5 minutes, final prayers, music and blessing, 5-10 minutes)

Prayers

O God,
You created us for love and by your love.
For your love in caring for us,
for your love in providing for us,
we give you thanks and praise.

For your love revealed in seeking us,
for your love revealed in meeting us,
for your love revealed in accepting us,
we give you thanks and praise.

For your love revealed in forgiveness,
for your love revealed in your saving power,
for your love revealed in the resurrection,
we give you thanks and praise.

Lord of the loving heart,
may mine be loving too.
Lord of the gentle hands,
may mine be gentle too.
Lord of the willing feet,
may mine be willing too.
So may I grow more like to thee
in all I say or do.

Hymn

Just as I am
Or: O love that will not let me go

The Blessing

God, in his love and forgiveness, accept you.
Christ, in his love and salvation, bring you home.
The Spirit, in his mighty power, restore and refresh you.
The grace of God, go with you now and always.

Recollect

Say throughout the week: 'I will arise and go to my Father.'
Remember, if you feel as if you are in a far country, it is you that
has moved, not God.

WEEK 7
Scorned and Rejected

Resources

Bring signs of neglect and indifference to the session, along with photographs of those who are scorned and rejected. The leader may like to bring symbols of the crucifixion: nails, a crown of thorns, a crucifix, or a painting of the crucifixion.

REALISE

(10 minutes)

Hymn

A man there lived in Galilee
Or: I danced in the morning
Or: There is a green hill
Or: O my Saviour lifted

After the music, keep a short time of silence and affirm that you are in the presence of God. Know that he loves you and gives you himself. Seek to be aware of the reality of God in your life. To live without regard to him is to live a lie.

The symbols of the crucifixion, or a crucifix, could be placed before the group at the start of these prayers:

On the Holy Cross I see
Jesus' hands nailed fast for me.
On the Holy Cross I see
Jesus' feet nailed fast for me.
Loving Jesus, let me be
still and quiet, close to thee.

Learning all thy love for me.
Giving all my love to thee.
(Source unknown)

For our failure to listen, Lord forgive us.
For our hardness of heart, Lord forgive us.
For our insensitivity to others, Lord forgive us.
For our fixed attitudes, Lord forgive us.
For our overcrowded lives, Lord forgive us.
For our overfilled days, Lord forgive us.
For our lack of concern, Lord forgive us.
For our unwillingness to change, Lord forgive us.
For our narrowness of vision, Lord forgive us.
For our turning away from you, Lord forgive us.

We adore you, O Christ, and we bless you,
For by your holy cross you have redeemed the world.

READ

(5-10 minutes)

Matthew 21:33-42 (or: Mark 12:1-12, or Luke 20:9-18)

Matthew 21:33-42

'Listen to another parable. There was a landowner who planted a vineyard, put a fence around it, dug a wine press in it, and built a watchtower. Then he leased it to tenants and went to another country. When the harvest time had come, he sent his slaves to the tenants to collect his produce. But the tenants seized his slaves and beat one, killed another, and stoned another. Again he sent other slaves, more than the first; and they treated them in the same way. Finally he sent his son to them, saying, "They will respect my son." But when the tenants saw the son, they said to themselves, "This is the heir; come let us kill him and get his inheritance." So they seized him, threw him out of the vineyard and killed him. Now when the owner of the vineyard comes, what will he do to those tenants?' They said to him, 'He will put those wretches to a miserable death, and lease the vineyard to other tenants who will give him the produce at the harvest time.' Jesus said to them, 'Have you never read in the scriptures: "The stone that the builders rejected has become the cornerstone; this was the Lord's doing, and it is amazing in our eyes"?'

RUMINATE

(in silence 10-15 minutes)

The scene is well known by all who listened to Jesus. Try to picture it. Grapes will grow almost anywhere. Vineyards were often on a terraced hillside. Around the vineyard is a quickset thorn hedge to keep animals and robbers out; it is necessary for protection. Inside the vineyard there is a tower, which is used as a lookout. The tower is also a safe place for the few belongings the labourers have. The workers will live in the tower during the times of planting, pruning and harvest. The vines need a lot of attention and good, clean ground if they are to produce a decent crop. Within the vineyard there is also a press for treading the grapes. This consists of two troughs, one higher than the other. The grapes are pressed in the higher trough and the juice is channelled into the lower one. Often vineyards were let out to tenant farmers. The landlord would come at harvest time to collect his dues, or he would send an agent. Payment would usually be a fixed amount of the crop, or a percentage of it. Sometimes the landlord was paid with money. At the time of Jesus, there was much unrest and hardship in the land. Many tenants were rebellious. The listeners would well understand the story, though all right-minded people would find it outrageous. In this instance, the tenants dare to set themselves against the servants. They beat one, they kill one, and they stone another. The landlord sends more servants, who receive the same treatment. Then the son is sent. Surely they will respect the son. Not these fellows! They know he is the son and heir and they seize him, throw him out of the vineyard, and kill him. When the owner comes, it will be in judgement. These wretches will lose all, even their lives. The vineyard will be given to those who will give the proper share of produce to the owner, to those who would have respected the son.

Most of the listeners would have agreed with the rights of this. There was something much deeper. They all knew Israel was referred to as the Vine of God (Psalm 80:8-13). They also knew that the vineyard had become a symbol of Israel's failure to live up to what God required (Isaiah 5:1-7). Jesus was talking about the relationship of the Church to God, and their rejection of him.

Jesus knew his own time was short. The people who had rejected the prophets were about to reject the son. The powers of the world want to get rid of him. He challenges their way of living, their power structures, their luxury, whilst others starve. He challenges their insensitivity to others. For this he will be condemned. The Jewish hierarchy are not comfortable with him. He asks about their dedication, their mission. He wants them to love, forgive and accept people as God does. For this he is condemned. Jesus knows opposition is mounting and his life is endangered.

He came in love and they will vent their hatred on him. He came to enrich their lives – they will strip him and condemn him. He came to set them free – they will fix him to a cross of wood. He came to give them life in all its fullness – they will put him to death. He will become the scorned and rejected.

We may like to say that it could never happen now. Yet it does, all the time. We still fail to give God his dues. He is as patient as ever and we still thrust him out of our lives. Think over this poem called 'Indifference' by Studdart Kennedy. You may like to replace the word 'Birmingham' by that of your own community:

When Jesus came to Birmingham
they simply passed him by.
They never hurt a hair of him
they simply let him die.
For men had grown more tender
and they would not give him pain.

They only just passed down the street
and left him in the rain.

Still Jesus cried, 'Forgive them, for they
know not what they do.'
And still it rained the wintry rain
that drenched him through and through.
The crowds went home and left the streets
without a soul to see.
And Jesus crouched against a wall
and cried for Calvary.

RESPOND

*(in two sections: 20 minutes group session, then 2 minutes silence, leading
into the next section)*

Look at the symbols of the crucifixion and the modern signs of
neglect and indifference. Talk about the scorned and the rejected
of society. Think upon the words of Jesus: 'As much as you did it
to the least of these, you did it to me.' In the quiet, think about the
mystery of the cross:

The God of love is scorned and rejected.
The Divine Healer suffers great pain.
He who brings us freedom, is fixed by nails.
The Lord of life is put to death.
The King of Heaven descends into hell.
Was there ever a love like this?

REST AND REJOICE

*(continue the silence for another 3-5 minutes; final prayers, music and
blessing, 5-10 minutes)*

Thanks be to thee, O Lord Jesus Christ,
for all the benefits which you have given us,
for all the pains and insults you have borne for us.
O merciful Redeemer, friend and brother,
may we know you more clearly,
love you more dearly,
and follow you more nearly
day by day.

(Richard of Chichester, 1197-1253)

Hymn

When I survey the wondrous cross
Or: My God, I love thee

The Blessing

May you find in Christ crucified
a sure ground for your faith,
a firm support for your hopes,
the assurance that sin is forgiven,
and the promise that life is eternal.
And the blessing of the holy Three
be upon you and your home now and for ever.

Recollect

Say often this week:

O my Saviour lifted
from the earth for me,
draw me, in thy mercy,
nearer unto thee.
(William Walsham How, 1823-97)

WEEK 8: EASTER DAY
Love Is Come Again

Resources

Bring symbols and signs of new life, new hope, of renewal and revival. Have a bowl of spring flowers placed in the room. Someone might like to create an Easter Garden with an empty tomb and a green hill with empty crosses on it. Someone else might like to create a poster with the words 'Christ is risen. Alleluia!' on it. Some brave soul might like to bring a photographic record of their life.

REALISE

(10 minutes)

Sing or listen to 'Now the green blade riseth', or 'Jesus Christ is risen today, Alleluia', or 'Low in the grave he lay'.

After the music, keep a short time of silence and affirm that you are in the presence of God. Know that he loves you and gives you himself. Seek to be aware of the reality of God in your life. To live without regard to him is to live a lie.

Jesus, stand among us
in your risen power;
let this time of worship
be a hallowed hour.

Breathe the Holy Spirit
into every heart;
bid the fears and sorrows
from each soul depart.

Thus with quickened footsteps
we pursue our way,
watching for the dawning
of eternal day.
(William Pennefather, 1816-73)

READ

(5-10 minutes)

John 12:23-36 and, in two parts, John 20:1-10, 11-18.

John 12:23-36

Jesus answered them, 'The hour has come for the Son of Man to be glorified. Very truly, I tell you, unless a grain of wheat falls into the earth and dies, it remains just a single grain; but if it dies, it bears much fruit. Those who love their life lose it, and those who hate their life in this world will keep it for eternal life. Whoever serves me must follow me, and where I am, there will my servant be also. Whoever serves me, the Father will honour.

'Now my soul is troubled. And what should I say – "Father, save me from this hour"? No, it is for this reason that I have come to this hour. Father, glorify your name.' Then a voice came from heaven, 'I have glorified it, and I will glorify it again.' The crowd standing there heard it and said that it was thunder. Others said, 'An angel has spoken to him.' Jesus answered, 'This voice has come for your sake, not for mine. Now is the judgement of this world; now the ruler of this world will be driven out. And I, when I am lifted up from the earth, will draw all people to myself.' He said this to indicate the kind of death he was to die. The crowd answered him, 'We have heard from the law that the Messiah remains for ever. How can you say that the Son of Man must be lifted up? Who is this Son of Man?' Jesus said to them, 'The light is with you for a little longer. Walk while you have the light, so that the darkness may not overtake you. If you walk in the darkness, you do not know where you are going. While you have the light, believe in the light, so that you may become children of light.'

John 20:1-10

Early on the first day of the week, while it was still dark, Mary Magdalene came to the tomb and saw that the stone had been removed from the tomb. So she ran and went to Simon Peter and the other disciple, the one whom Jesus loved, and said to them, 'They have taken the Lord out of the tomb, and we do not know where they have laid him.' Then Peter and the other disciple set out and went towards the tomb. The two were running together, but the other disciple outran Peter and reached the tomb first. He bent down to look in and saw the linen wrappings lying there, but he did not go in. Then Simon Peter came, following him, and went into the tomb. He saw the linen wrappings lying there, and the cloth that had been on Jesus' head, not lying with the linen wrappings but rolled up in a place by itself. Then the other disciple, who reached the tomb first, also went in, and he saw and believed; for as yet they did not understand the scripture, that he must rise from the dead. Then the disciples returned to their homes.

John 20:11-18

But Mary stood weeping outside the tomb. As she wept, she bent over to look into the tomb; and she saw two angels in white, sitting where the body of Jesus had been lying, one at the head and the other at the feet. They said to her, 'Woman, why are you weeping?' She said to them, 'They have taken away my Lord, and I do not know where they have laid him.' When she had said this, she turned around and saw Jesus standing there, but she did not know that it was Jesus. Jesus said to her, 'Woman, why are you weeping? Whom are you looking for?' Supposing him to be the gardener, she said to him, 'Sir, if you have carried him away, tell me where you have laid him, and I will take him away.' Jesus said to her, 'Mary!'

She turned and said to him in Hebrew, 'Rabbouni!' (which means Teacher). Jesus said to her, 'Do not hold on to me, because I have not yet ascended to the Father. But go to my brothers and say to them, "I am ascending to my Father and your Father, to my God and your God."' Mary Magdalene went and announced to the disciples, 'I have seen the Lord'; and she told them that he had said these things to her.

RUMINATE

(in silence 10-15 minutes)

There is a story of Lazy Jack, who didn't bury the grain, but kept it instead. His action endangered the lives of a whole community. Grain might look beautiful and golden, but it needs to be buried if it is to give life to many. This reading in John is not a parable but an analogy, comparing like with like. Jesus begins by talking about the Son of Man being glorified. Obviously, Jesus was aware of what was happening and that dangerous days lay ahead. The crowd were excited with the idea of glory and hoped for a conquest, perhaps even a driving out of the Romans who occupied the land. When Jesus started to talk of death they could not understand it, perhaps they did not even try to.

The grain of wheat has to be buried to give abundant life. If it is not broken down, it will not bear fruit. So often when we talk of 'breakdown', it is actually a chance for breakthrough into new life. If we are afraid of death, we will be afraid to live life to the full. The strange thing about us humans is that we are dying every day and in our death is our newness of life. You began life as a single cell, which had in inbuilt power to multiply. Today your body has about sixty million million cells and every single cell is alive and has its own force field. Each one of these cells is recognisable as your own and cannot belong to anyone else but you. You are an absolute miracle. Every second of every hour of every day of your life, about five million of your cells die. Even if you are a quick reader, while you have been reading these words, about fifty million of your living cells have departed from this life. Don't panic! The good news is that your body renews itself, and all the cells have been replaced by new cells. The body is in the business of death and resurrection. Every seven years or so, every single cell in your body will have died and been replaced by a new living cell. You are in a continual process of death and resurrection. I can happily say that I believe in the resurrection of the body.

If you've brought a photograph album of stages of your life, get it out and look at how you have changed over the years. Compare photographs with a seven- to ten-year gap and look at the changes; it is still the same you. The death of fifty million cells hasn't the power to destroy you. Surely if God can create such wonderful creatures, who are forever dying and rising, you can hardly doubt his power to give life beyond the grave. This theory about resurrection we know as a fact because of the resurrection of Jesus Christ.

In the battle between light and darkness, it would have seemed for a moment that darkness had triumphed when Jesus died. Try and picture the scene after the crucifixion: the death had come suddenly and burial had been rushed. Mary Magdalene, red-eyed through weeping and lack of sleep, wants to be near her beloved Jesus. It was the custom to visit a tomb for the three days following someone's death, because it was believed that the spirit of the dead person was there for those three days before departing. Because of the Sabbath and its restrictions, Mary has been unable to visit the tomb until now. It is very early, just before dawn, not long after three in the morning. Mary wonders who will roll the stone away and who will lift the heaviness in her heart. Her loved one is dead. Life will never be the same again. Evil has triumphed. When she arrives at the tomb, she finds that the stone is rolled away. This fills her with shock and alarm. Someone has broken into the tomb and stolen the body. Mary runs to tell Peter and John. How they must have loved her for waking them up before four in the morning! They run to the tomb. The young John outruns the older man and arrives at the tomb first, but does not go in. Peter, impetuous as ever, goes in. Then John enters. They see the linen clothes lying as if Jesus had just come through them. John begins to realise that something wonderful has happened – 'he saw and believed'. After this, the disciples go back home.

Mary returns to the tomb and weeps. The tears flow and blur her vision, though her mind is telling her not to weep. Looking at the empty clothes, she sees messengers from God who say to her, 'Why are you weeping?' She replies, 'I weep because I am separated from my loved one. They have taken away my Lord and I do not know where they have laid him.' As she is speaking, Jesus comes and asks her, 'Why are you weeping? For whom are you looking?' When certain events happen to us, our minds cannot take them in immediately. Perhaps Mary's tears blind her. She supposes him to be the gardener.

'Sir, if you have carried him away, tell me where you have laid him, and I will take him away.' Jesus simply replies, 'Mary.' Life for us all was never to be the same again. Mary sees and holds the risen Lord. This is no ghost, she can cling to him, she can hold him in her arms. Mary, who loved Jesus greatly, is the first to see the risen Lord. John, who was the beloved disciple, is the first to believe, even though at this point he has not seen.

Mary wants to stay hugging him for ever but such privilege brings responsibility. 'Mary, go and tell.' The dawn of a new era for us all had come. Mary goes back to the disciples – it is still very early – and simply says, 'I have seen the Lord.' Theories of life after death become a reality, for Christ is risen. Alleluia!

RESPOND

(in two sections: 20 minutes group session, then 2 minutes silence, leading into the next section)

Begin with a short silence and let everyone give thanks for the resurrection. Look at the Easter Garden and the signs of hope, growth and renewal. Place the poster in the middle of the group or pass it around. Let everyone in turn say, 'Christ is risen. Alleluia!'

The group might like to talk about the mystery of the human

body and the fact that every one of us shares in death and resurrection. The photograph album of someone's life might prove useful. Breakdown is often the point of breakthrough – what a relief this can be! Would any members of the group like to illustrate this from moments in their own life? John's Gospel seems to suggest that a relationship of love gives us a better opportunity of experiencing the resurrection. Would the group like to comment on this? Give thanks for the sharing and learning of the group over the last few weeks. Pray that we, in our turn, will be able to say, 'I have seen the Lord.'

Use these statements of St Augustine of Hippo to finish this section: 'We are Easter people' and 'Alleluia is our song'.

All shall be Amen and Alleluia.
We shall rest and we shall see,
we shall see and we shall know,
we shall know and we shall love,
we shall love and we shall praise.
Behold our end which is no end.
(St Augustine)

Before the silence, give thanks for growth, newness of life and the resurrection.

REST AND REJOICE

(continue the silence for another 3-5 minutes; final prayers, music and blessing, 5-10 minutes)

Rejoice, for
goodness is stronger than evil;
love is stronger than hate;
light is stronger than darkness;
life is stronger than death;
victory is ours through him who loves us.
(Desmond Tutu, An African Prayer Book,
Hodder and Stoughton, 1995)

Hymn

Thine be the glory
Or: Alleluia. Give thanks to the risen Lord

The Blessing

Christ, risen in glory,
scatter the darkness
from your heart and mind
and from the world,
that you may live in the fullness of life
and in awareness of his glorious kingdom.
And the blessing of God Almighty, the Father,
the Son and the Holy Spirit, be upon you now and for ever.

Recollect

Let him easter in us, be a dayspring to the dimness of us.
(Gerard Manley Hopkins)

I want to know Christ and the power of his resurrection.
(Philippians 3:10)

The group may like to use these prayers at the end of the sessions:

For our fellowship and friendship, we give you thanks and praise.
For our talents and our sharing, we give you thanks and praise.
For our growth and our learning, we give you thanks and praise.
For our faith and our hope, we give you thanks and praise.
For the firm foundation of Christ, we give you thanks and praise.

For your forgiveness and acceptance, glory to you, O Lord.
For your love in our redemption, glory to you, O Lord.
For your death and resurrection, glory to you, O Lord.
For your gift of life eternal, glory to you, O Lord.
For your presence with us always, glory to you, O Lord.

That we may rejoice in the Lord always, we ask in prayer.
That we may know him and the power of his resurrection,
  we ask in prayer.
That we may have life and life abundant, we ask in prayer.
That we may share in the glorious liberty of the children of God,
  we ask in prayer.
That we may dwell in him and he in us, we ask in prayer.

May the Christ, risen in glory, be known to dwell among us,
may the peace and joy of the risen Lord be upon each of us,
and the blessing of the Almighty, Father, Son and Holy Spirit
be with us, now and for ever. Amen.